About this book

Some potted plants climb, some trail, some are bushy, some flower and some are grown for their leaves. They will all last a very long time if you take care of them, and they will all help to make the rooms in which you grow them cheerful and bright.

You can ask for house plants as birthday or Christmas presents, and then you can grow new plants from the ones you have.

The beginning of this book shows you some of the plants you can grow, and explains where to grow them. Plants that are pictured in rooms with south-facing windows can also be grown in rooms with west-facing windows. Plants that are on the pages for north-facing windows will also do well in rooms with east-facing windows. The last part of the book gives step-by-step directions on how to grow and care for your plants and also how to make and do everything you see in the book.

Plants seem to grow better if they are grouped together, rather than grown on their own. You can try talking to them, too!

Designer : Pat Butterworth
Consultant : Rosemary Verey
Hydroponics consultant :
    James Scholto Douglas
Cover illustration by Barbara Firth
Artists' reference : The Smith Collection

© Walker Books Limited 1980
First published by Walker Books,
London, England

LIBRARY OF CONGRESS
CATALOG CARD NO. 80-82104
First American edition

Printed and bound in Italy by
Il Resto del Carlino, Bologna

ISBN 0-316-83206-5

Contents

The Potted Plant Book

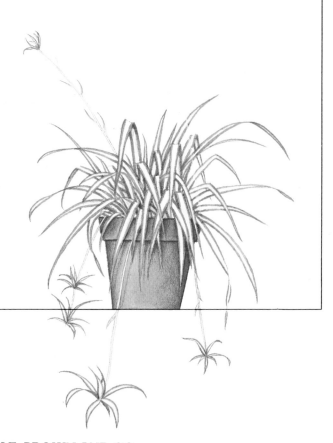

Written
by Sue Tarsky
Feature illustrations
by Will Giles
Activity illustrations
by Barbara Firth
Room illustrations
by Jane Wolsak

LITTLE, BROWN AND CO.

Boston

How to use this book

Symbols

Symbols are used on the step-by-step pages and on the chart (see p. 38) to show you which plants need direct light, indirect light or shade, when to water and when to feed. The chart also uses symbols to show you how easy or difficult it is to grow each plant. Remember to use the chart when you read about each plant.

Easy One star means a plant is easy to grow.

Not-so-easy Two stars mean a plant is not so easy to grow.

Difficult Three stars mean a plant is difficult to grow.

Shade A plant that needs shade will have this symbol near it.

Indirect light This means light that isn't full sunlight.

Direct light A plant that needs direct light has this symbol.

Feeding This is used to tell you when to feed.

Words to know

Bulb This is a bud covered with small, fat, scaly leaves that stays under the ground.

cross-section

Corm This is a short, fat stem with a bud on its end. It stays under the ground.

cross-section

Tuber A thick root or underground stem that stores food a plant needs in case of cold or drought.

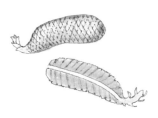

cross-section

Plantlet A small plant that grows on stems or runners of a parent plant.

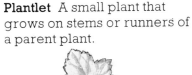

Offset A plant that grows on a parent plant and which can be cut off to make a new plant.

Rosette The circular shape in which some leaves grow.

Watering This shows you when to water well.

Watering This shows you when to water with a fine spray.

Composts
Different kinds of plants need to grow in different kinds of composts. This book tells you when to use peat or loam composts, when to use bulb fibre, and when to use sand. If no special kind is given, use an ordinary potting compost. You can always mix your own compost, but it's much easier, and safer for the plants, if you use bags of prepared compost that have all the correct items in them. You can buy the bags at a garden center.

Names
All plants have Latin names that botanists (plant scientists) use. If you want to know the Latin names for the plants in this book, look in the Index on p. 40. If a plant also has a common English name, it is the name you'll see used in this book.

Be sure that:
1. you always **ask an adult** to help you whenever it's advised in the book.
2. you always clean up after making or doing a project.

Parts of a plant
Seeds grow in the flowers.

A bud is a shoot that has leaves or flowers in it, ready to grow, from between a leaf and stem.

The stem supports the plant and its leaves, and carries food and water to all parts of the plant.

The plant breathes through its leaves, where food is made for the rest of the plant with the help of light.

The roots help hold the plant in place. They also take in food and water from the compost.

Basic care

House plants need certain amounts of heat, moisture in the air (called humidity), water, food and fresh air. Fumes from gas or coal fires can harm plants. Good soil is very important for healthy plants. Buy a bag of prepared potting compost from a garden center. Don't use common garden soil.

Some plants grow best in a warm temperature while others like a cool one. No plants like a big change in temperature from day to night. If your plants live with central heating, the air may be very dry. There are two easy ways to give your plants more humidity.

Stand your pot inside a larger pot. Pack peat between them. Water the peat and keep it moist all the time.

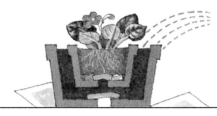

Rest your potted plant on a saucer of small pebbles and water. Make sure the water doesn't touch the pot.

Don't leave your plants in front of a window on cold winter nights unless there is a storm window or heavy curtains between the plant and the window. Never leave your plants between a window and a curtain at night. Don't put them on top of a radiator. They'll get too hot and dry.

All plants except those in flower will like short times outdoors in the summer, if the sun isn't too strong.

Buy food to give your plants after watering, or add liquid feed to their water. Read the directions on the bottle.

Plants breathe through their leaves, so they need to be clean. Wipe large leaves on both sides with a damp cloth.

Spray small leaves with clean water once a month, especially in the growing season.

Clean soft, hairy leaves with a small artist's brush. These kinds of leaves should not get wet.

Water from a tap is fine, but rain water is even better. You can put plants outdoors in short summer showers. Don't over-water house plants! It's the main reason house plants die. It's better to water well once a week than to water a little every day.

If you go away, put your plants around a bucket of water in a safe place. Tie a small stone to one end of a long wick. Drop it into the bucket. Put the wick's other end in the compost. Do one wick for each plant.

Ways to water

If the top of the compost looks dry, feel below it to see if it is dry all the way down. Water more in the summer and when leaves or buds are growing.

The water shouldn't be too hot or too cold. Remember that some plants need to be watered from the bottom, others from the top. Don't over-water!

You will need
Large pretty container
Brick
Watering can with long spout
Large bowl
Bag of peat from a garden
center
Bucket of water

Put a brick into the pretty container. Put your potted plant on top of the brick and water it. Extra water is soaked up by the brick and then by the air.

Pack peat all round some potted plants inside a bowl. Peat keeps the plants moist so you don't have to water too often. You can also hide your chipped clay pots.

Use a watering can that has a long spout to water plants with soft, hairy leaves. The end of the spout goes under the leaves. This kind of leaf should never get wet.

Plants with flowers or leaves that may be harmed by water can be watered from the bottom (see p. 10). Put water in the saucer. The compost soaks up the water it needs.

After about half an hour, empty the saucer so that the roots don't start to rot. Too much water in the compost forces out the air that the roots need.

If you can see that a plant is very dry and that the compost doesn't touch the sides of the pot, put it into a bucket. Add water until it just covers the top of the pot.

You will see air bubbles coming up to the top of the water. The water is forcing out the air in the compost.

When the bubbles stop coming up, take out the pot. Put it in a sink to let the extra water drain away. Air goes back into the compost as the water drains away.

Light and temperature

Choose your plants for the kind of light and temperature you will be giving them. They won't grow well if you put them in a place that isn't suited to them, and you can't change the heating and light in a room to suit your plants' needs.

There are big temperature and light changes even within one room. It may look bright to you, but the further away from a window you put a plant, the less light it is going to get. Plants need light to live – they can't grow without it. Certain plants need more light than others. The chart on p. 38 shows what light a plant needs.

Some windows get more daylight, and stronger light, than others. A window that faces south gives the most light. Direct summer sunlight is too hot for many plants.

East-facing windows get a lot of sun in the morning and good indirect light all through the day. Plants that like shade will grow well in eastern light as long as you don't keep them right in front of the windows.

West-facing windows stay lighter later in the day than other windows. The summer sun may be too strong for some plants. Grow plants that need good, indirect light here.

A north window gives less light but it is constant. Many house plants will do well here.

Good indirect light is usually better than hot, strong light. You may have to move your plants closer to the window in the winter for more light (be careful of cold drafts) and then move them away, in the summer. Always turn the pots around so each side of the plant gets its share of light. Otherwise the plant will lean towards the light instead of growing straight up.

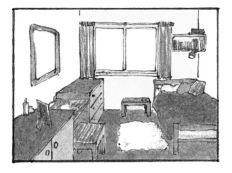

Some plants with variegated leaves (marked with contrasting colors), Daffodils, Hyacinths, Chrysanthemums, Geraniums and cacti can grow in full light.

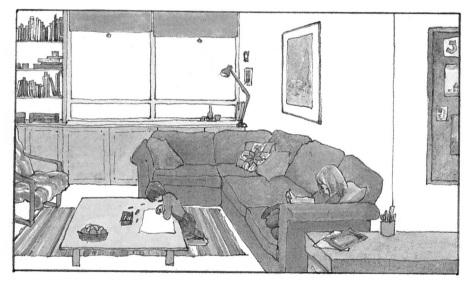

Peperomia, Swiss Cheese Plant, Rubber Tree and Impatiens can grow in west window light. Plants with dark green leaves can grow in northern light.

A living room may be cooler at night than in the day, and the air may be dry. Plants here may need humidity (see p. 4).

A bedroom is usually cooler than a living room There is usually enough humidity and light. If the room is cool, don't water as much. The compost stays moist longer.

A kitchen and bathroom have high humidity.

The amount of light affects temperature. Put a plant where its needs will be met.

If you are lucky enough to have a sun room with big glass windows, you can grow many kinds of plants in it because the light is good. Be sure there is good fresh air in the summer, and enough humidity. Protect your plants from hot summer sun. The kinds of plants you can grow depends on the room's temperature in the winter, too.

South-facing bedroom

A south-facing window gives good light (see p. 6). Some plants will have to be moved away from the window, especially in the summer when the sun is very strong.

The Shrimp Plant is a bushy plant whose leaves stay green all year round. It has white flowers from April to December. The plant grows to about 38cm.

If you look at a Prayer Plant at night, you'll see that the leaves actually fold upright. The plant grows to about 20cm in height.

The Christmas Cactus needs to be potted in a compost of one part sand, one part peat and two parts loam. You can buy these items at a garden center. You can hang the pot when the plant grows red flowers from November to January (see p. 32) Spray it when it is flowering.

The Partridge-breasted Aloe flowers in March. It is popular because of its green and white leaves, which grow in a shape called a rosette. Never water in this plant's rosette.

Grow the Golden Barrel in a compost with coarse sand. You can buy special compost that's already mixed for all your cacti. This cactus almost never flowers indoors.

The *Echinocereus pectinatus* grows quickly, to about 20cm. It flowers in the summer.

The *Echeveria gibbiflora* leaves have little bubbles on them and grow in a rosette.

Grow the Jade Plant for its thick leaves. It almost never flowers indoors.

You can grow a Spider Plant and Speedy Jenny almost anywhere. They both do well in hanging pots. Pinch out the growing stem tips of Speedy Jenny to make it bushy (see p. 28).

A Philodendron is easy to grow, and will grow to 180cm.

Shrimp Plant

Christmas Cactus

Prayer Plant

Spider Plant

Speedy Jenny

Philodendron

Partridge-breasted Aloe

Jade Plant

Echinocereus pectinatus

Golden Barrel

Echeveria gibbiflora
'Carunculata'

9

North-facing bedroom

A north-facing bedroom gives steady light, though not as much as a south window (see p. 6).

A Weeping Fig can grow to about 180cm indoors. It could grow to 12m in a jungle! It needs humidity (see p. 4). The pointed leaves get darker as they grow older.

The Cyclamen needs to be kept cool and humid when it is flowering, from November to March. As leaves and flowers die, twist off the whole stem from the plant with your fingers. Water this plant from the bottom (see p. 5) and don't keep it in drafts.

Chrysanthemums are grown as house plants for their flowers, which can be in lots of different colors and shapes. When the flowers die, cut them off straight away. Cut down the flower stems and the plant will make new shoots which you can use as cuttings before you throw the whole plant away.

African Violets aren't very easy to grow, but once you find the correct place, you'll have flowers in many colors that last a long time. The leaves are hairy, so don't let water get on them (see p. 5). They need good humidity (see p. 4). If a leaf or flower dies, twist off the whole stem from the plant. Repot plants between May and August in compost with peat. Don't over-water.

Piggy-back Plants grow plantlets on the base of their older leaves! Grow them in an all-peat compost.

A Kangaroo Vine can grow quickly almost anywhere, even in a hanging pot. Pinch out the growing tips if you want it to be bushy (see p. 28).

A Cast Iron Plant can grow in drafts, fumes, shade and dry air. It doesn't like to be left standing in water.

Weeping Fig

Cyclamen

Kangaroo \

Cast Iron Plant

Chrysanthemum

African Violet

Piggy-back Plant

11

South-facing kitchen

A kitchen is good for plants that need high humidity.

A Watermelon Peperomia has silver stripes on its leaves and reddish stems. It can grow to about 23cm in height.

An Aluminum Plant has silver marks on its leaves. Pinch out growing shoots in the spring to make it bushy (see p. 28). It can grow to about 30cm in height.

The Amaryllis is a bulb that will flower more than once indoors (see p. 21 for planting and growing). It flowers from December to May, in red, pink and white. Plant bulbs from November to February but keep them in good indirect light, unlike other bulbs. Water well from when leaves show till when they turn yellow, after flowering. Pull off the leaves when they dry up, and put the pots in a cool, dark place till November.

Tulips are bulbs, too. Plant them the same way as Hyacinths (see p. 21), but keep them in a cool, dark place until the shoots grow. Then put the pot in a cool place with good indirect light. Water well. When the leaves are growing well, put the pot in a warmer room. When the flowers die, treat the same way as Hyacinths.

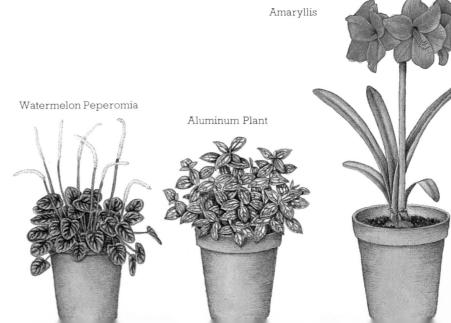

Amaryllis

Watermelon Peperomia

Aluminum Plant

Tulip

Daffodil

Hyacinth

Wandering Jew

Plant Daffodils in the same way as Tulips, but don't give them as much water. Put their pot into a warmer room when the flower buds are growing well.

The Achimenes flowers from June to October. Cut back the stems and store the tubers in sand after flowering. Repot in peat the next spring.

The Wandering Jew is easy to grow and does well in a hanging pot. Pinch out the growing tips to make it bushy (see p. 28).

The Carrot top and Pineapple are both easy to grow hydroponically (see p. 35).

Pineapple

Achimenes

Carrot

North-facing bathroom

A bathroom can be humid, too.

You can grow the Delta Maidenhair fern in a hanging pot if you want. It needs humidity and a peat compost.

The Asparagus Fern is really part of the Lily family, and not a fern at all, though it looks like one! It's easy to grow if the air isn't too dry. The long stems will hang or you can train them to climb.

The Kangaroo Vine is usually grown so that it climbs, which it does quickly and easily (see p. 10).

Queen's Tears is a bromeliad. These plants grow their leaves in a rosette. The Queen's Tears has upright rosettes of narrow leaves. Keep water inside the rosettes when the plant is growing from May to September. It has small, tube-shaped flowers that are blue, green and yellow from the winter to early summer. Each rosette flowers once and grows offsets, which you can cut away and put in their own pots. The parent plant then slowly dies. Keep Queen's Tears in as small a pot as you can without it falling over, in a peat compost. It can grow to 45cm.

Queen's Tears

Delta Maidenhair Fern

Asparagus Fern

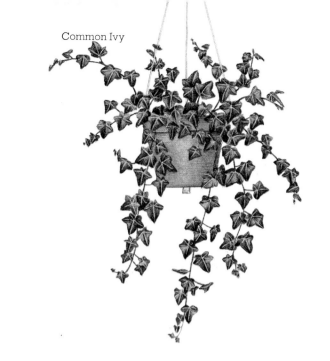
Common Ivy

There are many different kinds of Common Ivy, and they are all easy to grow, even in a cold room. They can hang down or climb on a support. Clean the leaves with a damp cloth (see p. 4).

You can grow a Date Palm from a stone of a date after you eat the fruit. Put a fresh stone in a pot of potting compost in the spring. Keep it in good indirect light in a warm room. Water well through the spring and summer, and just enough to stop it drying out in the winter. Pot it on every spring till it's about 60cm tall, and then as needed (see p. 23). It can grow to 180cm!

Date Palm

Kangaroo Vine

South-facing living room

A living room will probably be warmer than a bedroom and the air may be dry. The south window is hot in the summer.

The Rubber Tree is grown for its big, shiny, dark green leaves. Remember to clean them (see p. 4). It can grow to 180cm in a room. If your plant does grow tall, keep it on its own or no one will notice plants near it. If it grows too big, you can make a new plant from it (see p. 25).

The Impatiens is easy to grow in any place where there is good light. Give it shade in the spring and summer. It flowers almost all year round in pink, red or white. If you cut back the top shoots in the spring, it will grow bushy (see p. 28). It can grow to about 50cm in height, and should be in an all-peat compost.

An Ivy-leaved Geranium has leaves that look rather like Common Ivy, on long trailing stems. It is easy to grow, and will give you big pink, red, purple or white flowers. It may want to be in a cool room in the winter while it is resting, and likes fresh air in the summer.

There are lots of different kinds of Coleus. They are grown for their brightly colored leaves, which have markings on them. The plant needs full sunlight or the colors fade. It's easy to grow. Pinch out the central growing tips in early spring to make it bushy. Spray it in the summer (don't overwater), and it should grow to about 50cm.

The Chinese Hibiscus is a bushy plant with big flowers in yellow, pink, red or white. Grow it in an all-peat compost and spray it in the summer. It can grow to 180cm, but you should cut it back in spring.

Rubber Tree

Impatiens

Coleus

Ivy-leaved Geranium

Chinese Hibiscus

North-facing living room

A north-facing room gets constant light, so your plants should grow well here if they aren't too far from the window and if the air isn't too dry.

A Cape Primrose is grown for its flowers, clusters of reds, purples and white, from May to October. The crinkly leaves grow in a rosette. Give it fresh air in the summer, and humidity if the room is dry (see p. 4).

The flower of the Urn Plant lasts a long time. When it starts to grow it is pink, but you can watch it change slowly to blue as it gets older. As with all bromeliads (see p. 14), keep the rosette of leaves, called the 'vase', filled with water from May to September. It should be dry in winter. Grow the Urn Plant in a small pot of all-peat compost. It can live in dry air, shade and cool temperatures. It will grow flowers and offsets. When the offsets have roots, cut them off and plant them in their own pots (see p. 22). Keep the pots in a warm place until the offsets are well-rooted. Be careful of the spines on the edges of the leaves!

A Begonia rex is grown for its crinkly leaves with markings in many different colors. You may have to give the Begonia humidity (see p. 4). Use an all-peat compost.

A Prayer Plant (see p. 8) and Common Ivy (see p. 14) will also grow well here.

The Swiss Cheese Plant has cuts and holes in its big, thick leaves. Be sure you clean them (see p. 4). It also has aerial roots that it will push into a climbing stick for support (see p. 29). Grow it in a large pot of all-peat compost, spray it in spring and summer, and it may grow up to 6m after many years.

Urn Plant

Cape Primrose

Common Ivy

Swiss Cheese Plant

Begonia rex

Prayer Plant

19

Growing from seed

It's easy to sow seeds, but it isn't easy to help them grow into strong, healthy plants. The seeds must have very high humidity and the seedlings must have very good indirect light if you are to end up with plants worth keeping.

Remember that there are other ways to multiply your plants (see p. 24).

You will need
Old newspapers
Pots
Pieces of broken clay pots (crocks)
Garden trowel or old spoon
Seed compost and seed packets from a garden center
Sand
Large, clear plastic bag
Sharp scissors

1. Cover the drainage holes with crocks
Fill the pot to about 2cm from the top with compost.

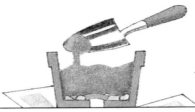

2. Sow the seeds very thinly with your fingers. It may help to mix a little sand in the seed packet first.

3. Cover the seeds with a very thin layer of sand. The seeds should be just covered.

4. Put the pot in about 2cm of water in a sink. Let the compost soak up the water until the top is dark.

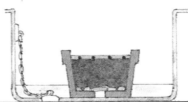

5. Put the pot in a saucer and let the extra water drain away for about two hours.

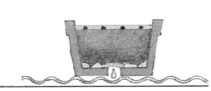

6. Carefully cover the pot with the plastic bag. It must never touch the seeds or the seedlings.

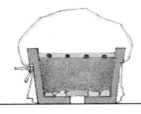

7. Put the pot, covered with plastic, in a warm, dark cupboard.

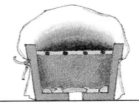

8. If drops of water form inside the plastic, take it off, turn it inside out and put it back. Do this daily.

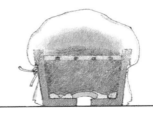

9. When the seedlings grow, take off the plastic bag and move the pot to good, warm, indirect light.

10. Cut weak seedlings with scissors at compost level. It will help seedlings grow if they are above a radiator.

11. Repot each seedling to its own pot when you can pick it up by the leaves without harming it (see p. 23).

Planting bulbs

You can buy bulbs at the end of your summer vacation. They must be specially prepared ones that can be forced to flower indoors in the winter.

Pot them from the end of September to the beginning of October, so they flower for Christmas and in January. Bulbs can be forced only once.

You will need
Old newspapers
Bulbs and bulb fibre from a garden center
Bucket of water
Bowl without drainage holes
Garden trowel or old spoon
Watering can
Stakes and string
Sharp scissors

1. Soak the fibre overnight in the bucket. Squeeze it out so it's moist but not wet.

2. Use the trowel to fill the bowl to about 8cm from the top with the fibre.

3. Gently but firmly put the bulbs into the fibre, tips pointed up. Leave a space of 2.5cm between each bulb.

4. Add more fibre around the bulbs until only their tips are showing.

5. Leave the bowl in a cool, dark place for about eight weeks. Water the fibre so it doesn't dry out.

6. For Hyacinths, look for the tops of the flower buds. Other kinds of bulbs need different care.

7. When you see the tops of the buds, put the bowl in a cool place with indirect light.

8. Turn the bowl every day so the stems grow straight up.

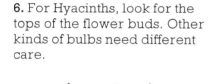

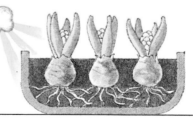

9. When the flowers open, leave the bowl in indirect light.

10. Water as needed. Tie the stems loosely to stakes if needed.

11. Cut dead flower stems. When the leaves die down, plant the bulbs in someone's garden to flower next year.

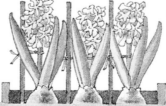
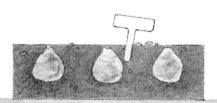

Potting and repotting

If you get plants that aren't in pots, you'll have to pot them. When you see roots through the drainage hole, take the plant and its compost ball out of the pot to see if it needs a larger pot. If it doesn't, and you put the plant back into the same pot but with new compost, it's called 'repotting'.

You will need
Old newspapers
Pot with crocks over drainage holes (plastic pots don't need their holes covered)
Potting compost (if possible, same kind as plant has been growing in)
Garden trowel or old spoon
Sharp knife
Watering can

1. Put a layer of compost into the pot so that the plant will be about 2.5cm from the top of the pot.

2. Rest the plant on the compost. Add more compost around it. Firm around the edges of pot. Water well.

1. Ask an adult to move the knife between the compost and the pot to loosen the compost ball.

2. Turn the pot upside down with the base of the stem between two fingers and your palm flat on the compost.

3. Tap the rim of the pot sharply against a table top so that the compost ball comes out in one piece.

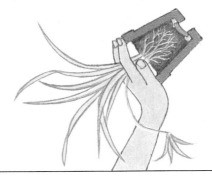

4. If the roots don't wrap around, put a layer of new compost in the pot. Rest the compost ball on it.

5. Fill in around the plant with more compost. Firm around the edges. Water well.

6. If the roots do wrap around themselves in the compost ball, it's time to pot on (see p. 23).

Potting on

If you put a plant into a larger pot than it's been in, with new compost, it's called 'potting on'. You do this when your plant has grown and the roots need more space. You can pot on at any time of the year, but be sure to look at the roots in the spring, when many house plants are growing after their winter rest.

You will need
Old newspapers
Sharp knife
Pot – same kind (plastic or clay) plant has been growing in but one size larger
Bucket of water
Pieces of crocks
Potting compost – same kind plant has been growing in
Watering can

1. Soak new clay pots in the bucket overnight. If you use old pots; clean them well first.

2. Cover the drainage holes with the broken crockery so water can drain away without compost clogging the holes.

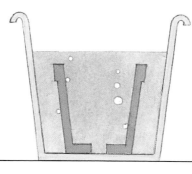

3. Put in enough compost so the compost ball will be about 2cm from the top of the pot when you put it in.

4. Take the plant out of the pot it's been growing in (see p. 22).

5. Put the plant and its compost ball on to the compost in its new pot.

6. Fill in with more compost. It should come to the same height on the stem as where the old compost was.

7. Gently firm the compost around the edge of the pot.

8. Water well. Put the plant in shade for about three days. Water less than usual until the roots take hold.

Multiplying your plants

There are different ways to grow new plants from many of the plants you have. Increasing your plants this way is called 'propagation'. It's a good way to add to your plants because it doesn't cost much. There are usually one or two ways to propagate a plant. Be sure you know the correct ways for your plants.

You will need
Old newspapers
Clean pot filled with potting compost for each new plant (remember to cover the drainage holes with crocks)
Garden trowel or old spoon
Paper clip
Sharp scissors
Watering can
Glass jar filled with water

1. Plantlets Put each young plant into a new pot. If it doesn't stay down, make a loop from a clip to hold it.

2. Cut the runner of the parent plant with scissors when the plantlet is growing well.

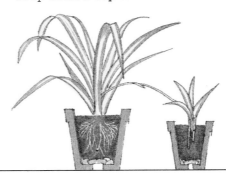

1. Division Take the plant from its pot. Gently pull it apart between the roots and stems where it is branching.

2. Put each whole new plant into its own pot (see p. 22).

3. Water the plants well and keep them in shade until they are growing well.

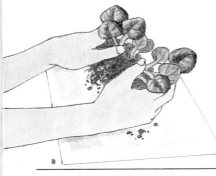

1. Stem cutting Cut off a growing tip about 10cm long below the leaf joint. Take off the lower leaves.

2. Put the stem into a jar of water. You can watch the roots grow.

3. When the roots look strong, plant the stem in a pot (see p. 22). Water. Keep in shade until it's growing well.

When a plant grows too tall and starts to lose its bottom leaves, you can air layer it to make a shorter, new plant. After a while, the old plant may grow new shoots.

Air layering is good for the Rubber Tree, the Swiss Cheese Plant and the Philodendron. Do this in the spring or the summer.

You will need
Old newspapers
Sharp knife
Sphagnum moss from a garden center
Strong string
Clear plastic
Clean pot filled with potting compost (cover the drainage holes with crocks)
Garden trowel or old spoon

1. Ask an adult to make an upward slanting cut about 2cm long, almost half-way through the stem below the leaves.

2. Carefully push some moss into the cut to stop it from closing.

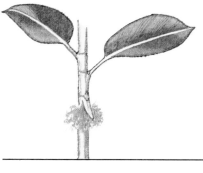

3. Make a ball of moss around the cut in the stem and tie it in place.

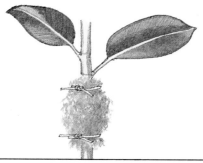

4. Put the plastic over the moss ball and tie it securely round the stem at the top and bottom.

5. Take off the plastic when you can see new roots growing through the moss ball.

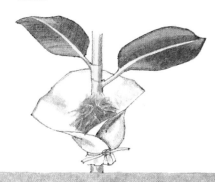

6. Ask an adult to carefully cut through the stem just below the new roots.

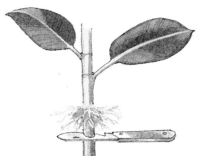

7. Put your new plant into a pot that is about 2cm bigger than the root ball (see p. 23).

You can propagate some plants from leaf cuttings. For some plants, you can use just their leaves. For other plants, you use their leaves and stems. For still other plants, you cut up their leaves into small pieces. Leaf cuttings are an easy way to multiply your plants. The chart on p. 38 tells you ways to propagate.

You will need
Old newspapers
Sharp scissors
Glass jar ⅔ full of water
Paper clip
Watering can
Clean pot filled with potting compost or sand for each new plant (cover holes)
Garden trowel or old spoon
Sharp knife
Tiny pebbles
Small stakes
Clear plastic bag

1. With the scissors, cut off a leaf and about 5cm of its stem.

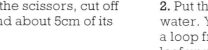

2. Put the leaf into the jar of water. You may have to make a loop from a clip to hold the leaf upright.

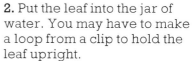

3. Keep up the water level. In about six weeks, you will see roots and small plantlets growing.

4. When the plantlets are big enough to handle, cut them from the parent leaf.

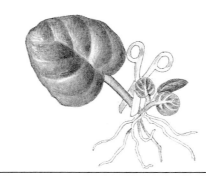

5. Put each plantlet into its own small pot of compost (see p. 22).

1. Ask an adult to cut a leaf into pieces about 2cm across with the knife.

2. Hold down the pieces on damp sand with tiny pebbles. Put stakes in the pot and cover it with the plastic.

3. When the new plantlets that grow have two good leaves, put each plantlet into its own pot of compost.

Some hairy-leaved plants, such as African Violet, Peperomia and Begonia rex, can grow new plants from a leaf and its stem in compost and sand.

You will need
Old newspapers
Sharp scissors
Garden trowel or old spoon
Shallow pot of compost with 5cm layer of sand on top
Clean pot filled with potting compost for each new plant (cover drainage holes)
Watering can
Stakes
String
Clear plastic bag
Sharp knife

1. With the scissors, cut off a leaf and its stem where it joins the main stalk.

2. Make a hole in the pot of compost and sand and put in the leaf. Tie it loosely to a stake. Water well.

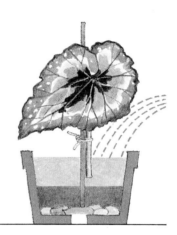

3. Put stakes in the pot and cover it with the plastic. The bag must not touch the leaf.

4. Take off the bag when the plantlets are big enough to handle. **Ask an adult** to cut off the plantlets.

5. Put each plantlet into its own small pot of compost (see p. 22).

Training a 'tree'

You can train a bushy plant to grow into a 'tree' by pinching out certain growing shoots. This is really a kind of pruning – cutting back some growing parts to control the size and shape of a plant and help keep it flowering. The more shoots you pinch out, the bushier a plant will be.

You will need
Old newspapers
One-stemmed plant about
1·2cm tall in a 7.5cm pot
30cm stake
Soft, strong string
12.5cm pot ready for planting
Garden trowel or old spoon
75cm stake
Potting compost
20cm pot ready for planting

1. Put the 30cm stake next to the plant. Tie them together with string (not tightly) so the knot touches the stake.

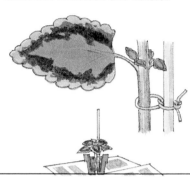

2. When the plant grows to 25cm tall, pot it on to a 12.5cm pot (see p. 23). Tie it to a 75cm stake.

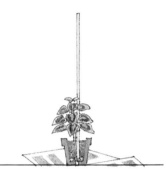

3. Pinch out all but the top side shoots. They have two small leaves that look the same all along the stalk.

4. Pinch out the growing tip and one side leaf next to it. Tie up the other side leaf to make the new growing tip.

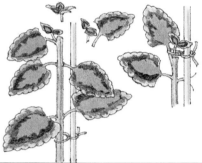

5. When the plant grows to about 60cm tall, pot it on to a 20cm pot. Tie it to the 75cm stake again.

6. Pinch out the main growing tip.

7. Pinch out the tips of the new shoots that grow. This helps the plant to branch more, and get even bushier.

8. Be patient! If you do this for about a year, the side leaves will fall off and you will have a 'tree'.

Making a climbing stick

You can make a climbing stick for some of your vines. Once they start to climb, they may grow more quickly and their leaves may grow bigger than they did when they were hanging down. Plants that grow aerial roots, such as the Swiss Cheese Plant, will be able to push their roots into the moss.

You will need
Old newspapers
20cm x 60cm piece of plastic mesh with holes of about 12.5mm from hardware store
Damp sphagnum moss from garden center
Strong string
Large-eyed sewing needle
Garden trowel or old spoon
20cm pot ready for planting
Potting compost
Flexible wire
Watering can

1. Lay the plastic mesh down. Put moss all along the inside curve of the mesh.

2. Roll the mesh so the long ends overlap. Stitch them tightly closed with the needle and string.

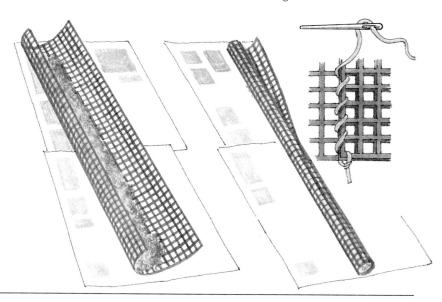

3. Hold the stick near the edge of the pot with one hand. With your other hand, fill in the pot with compost.

4. Pot the plant next to the stick. Bend wire around the stem and stick to keep them together (not too tightly).

5. Add more moss to the top of the stick if it's needed. Water the moss to keep it damp.

Making a bottle garden

A bottle garden is fun to make and easy to take care of. You only need to water the plants in it about once a year! Be sure that the plants you put inside all need the same amounts of heat and light, and that none of them grows too big. Plants with pretty leaves do better in bottle gardens than flowering plants.

You will need
Clean, dry, glass bottle
Heavy paper and tape
Small pebbles or stones
Potting compost and plants
Old spoon, fork and empty
cotton spool, all tied to long
sticks
2 sticks tied together
Plug of cork or cotton

1. Make a funnel from the paper to fit inside the neck of the bottle.

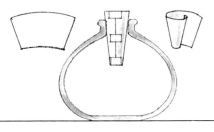

2. Pour a layer of pebbles 2.5cm deep along the bottom.

3. Pour in a layer of compost about 10cm deep. Spread it evenly with the spoon.

4. Use the spoon to make one hole in the compost for each plant you want to put in.

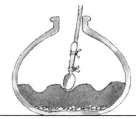

5. Use the two sticks as tongs to put in the plants, the tallest in the center.

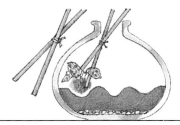

6. Carefully fork the compost gently over the roots.

7. Use the spool to firm the compost around the plants. Spray the plants lightly.

8. Put a plug into the bottle. Drops of water will form on the inside of the glass.

9. When the drops of water are gone, put the bottle in good indirect light.

10. Water in about two months, and then only about once a year, with a fine spray.

11. Ask an adult to cut off dead leaves with a razor blade tied to a stick.

Making a terrarium

A terrarium is any open or closed clear container that you grow plants in. It can be an old glass fish tank, or a lightweight plastic case that doesn't break easily. It's easy to make because you can put your hands inside the opening of the case. Choose plants with the same needs, that won't grow too big.

You will need
Old newspapers
Large plastic fish tank
Small pebbles or stones
Charcoal from garden center
Potting compost
Garden trowel or old spoon
Plants (see p. 22 to learn how to take them from pots)
Watering spray

1. Clean your case well with soap and water. Let it dry completely.

2. Put the case where you want it after you plant it, in good indirect light. Put down a layer of pebbles 2cm deep along the bottom.

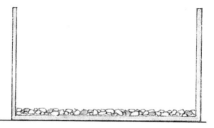

3. Put down a layer of charcoal about 5cm deep. If your terrarium is small, the layers should not be this deep.

4. Put down a layer of compost about 10cm deep. The compost doesn't have to be flat – it can be higher at one end if you like.

5. Use the spoon to make one hole in the compost for each plant you want to put in. Leave some space in between for the plants to grow.

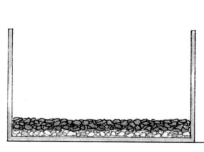
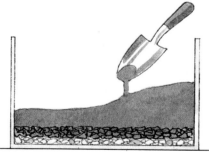

6. Carefully put the plants into the holes. Small plants that like warmth and humidity should grow well in a terrarium.

7. Gently firm the compost around each plant. If your terrarium is open, water with a fine spray from time to time.

8. If your terrarium is airtight, you need to water the plants with a spray only about once a year.

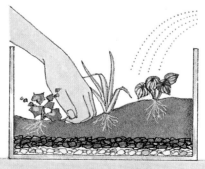

Making a hanging pot

A hanging pot is a perfect place to grow your trailing plants. You can buy pots specially made for hanging, or make a pot you have into a hanging one. Don't hang it too high – you have to be able to reach it for watering. Plants in hanging pots need more water and food than they do in other pots.

You will need
Old newspapers
Clay or plastic pot with broken crockery in it
Potting compost and plants
Garden trowel or old spoon
3 small stakes
Clean aluminum pie tin
Sharp scissors
7 long pieces of very strong string
Hook or bracket and screws
Watering can

1. You can hang up a pot that has trailing plants already growing in it, or you can put some plants into a pot. Partly fill a clean pot with compost.

2. Put trailing plants in the pot towards the edge. Firm the compost around them. Add more compost to fill in around them.

3. Use the spoon to make holes in the compost in the center of the pot.

4. Put in upright plants and firm the compost around them.

5. Ask an adult to punch three small holes at equal spaces from each other around the rim of the tin, using the scissors.

6. Put in stakes at equal spaces around the pot. Put the tin under the pot. Thread three strings through the holes. Tie the ends of each string around a stake.

7. Tie a string under the rim of the pot around the outside. Knot it. Tie the ends of three more strings to this one at equal spaces. Knot all the other ends together.

8. Ask an adult to screw a hook in the ceiling or a bracket on the wall. Hang up your pot.

Making a dish garden

You can grow some of your small plants together in a shallow dish. The plants must need the same amounts of light and humidity, and like the same temperature.

If the plants grow too big, take them out and put them in their own pots (see p. 22). Put some of your other small plants in their places in the dish.

You will need
Old newspapers
Old dish about 7.5cm deep
Small pebbles or stones
Potting compost
Garden trowel or old spoon
Plants (to take them from their pots see p. 22)
Pretty rock

1. Clean your dish well with soap and water. Let it dry completely.

2. Put down a layer of pebbles 1cm deep. The pebbles give your plants good drainage, since there are no drainage holes in the dish.

3. Use the trowel to put down a layer of compost, not too deep.

4. Take your plants out of their pots (see p. 22).

5. Use the trowel to make one hole in the compost for each plant you want to put in.

6. Put each plant into a hole. Firm the compost around the plants gently.

7. Put the dish in a sink of water. The water should just cover the dish. Air bubbles will rise to the top of the water. When they stop, take out the dish.

8. Let the extra water drain away for about an hour by putting something under one end of the dish to tilt it.

What is hydroponics?

Hydroponics is growing plants without soil. You put them into a 'medium', which can be sand, a mixture of sand and vermiculite, sand and perlite, sand and fine gravel, even sand and washed cinders or charcoal. It should always be damp. Your plants need good drainage. Feed them with a 'nutrient'.

You will need
Old newspapers
Clay or plastic pot
Cork to fit drainage hole
Small, clean pebbles
Cup for measuring
Garden trowel or old spoon
Bags of whichever medium you choose, from a garden center
Plants
Watering can
Saucer or tray
Prepared nutrient from a garden center

1. Put a plug into the drainage hole from the bottom. Don't push it in too hard – you need to take it out from time to time.

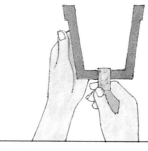

2. Put down a thin layer of pebbles for good drainage.

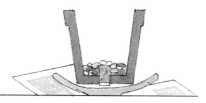

3. Mix two cups of sand to three cups of your other item, to make your medium.

4. Use the trowel to fill the pot to about 12.5cm from the top with the medium. Firm it down.

5. Use the trowel to dig a hole in the medium for your plant.

6. Get your plant ready to go into the medium (see p. 35). Compost must never be on plants grown in hydroponics.

7. Water until the medium is damp. If you over-water, take out the plug until the extra water drains away. Then put the plug in again.

8. Read directions that come with the nutrient. Feed your plants about twice a week. Wash old food through with clean water once a month.

Hydroponic plants

You can grow just about anything hydroponically. You may have already grown something this way, and not known it. If you grow a plant in water, it's a kind of hydroponics. You'll find that your plants may grow more quickly in a hydroponic medium than they do in compost. Remember to feed them.

You will need
Old newspapers
Carrot
Sharp knife
Shallow bowl
Watering can
Pineapple
Pots ready for planting with plug and medium
Potted plant
Cotton swab
Disinfectant that won't harm plants
Garden trowel or old spoon

1. Carrot Ask an adult to cut off the top of a fresh Carrot. Put the top into a shallow bowl of water, cut side down, on a sunny window sill.

2. Add water so the bowl doesn't dry out. You can watch the top grow. leaves that look like ferns.

1. Pineapple Ask an adult to cut off the top of a Pineapple, below the first row of pips on the outside skin.

2. Ask an adult to cut away some of the soft flesh underneath the top. Let the top dry out for two days.

3. Plant the top in a hydroponic pot. Keep it in a warm place with good indirect light and you can grow a new Pineapple plant.

1. House plants Take a plant out of its pot (see p. 22). Hold it under slowly running water till all the compost runs off the stem and roots.

2. Dip a cotton swab into a mixture of water and disinfectant (follow directions on the bottle). Wipe it over the roots.

3. Put your plant into a hydroponic pot (see p. 34).

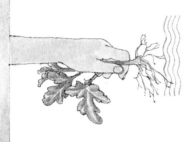

Pests and problems

If your plants get the water, light, humidity and temperature they need, they are less likely to be attacked by pests or diseases. But sometimes a plant does get attacked.

You can buy chemicals from a garden center to spray on unhealthy plants. There are different chemicals for many of the bugs and diseases, so ask before you buy. Don't mix the chemicals or spray the plants yourself! **Ask an adult** to do it for you. Spray about 30cm from a plant. Be sure there is fresh air in the room. Take a plant outdoors in the summer to spray it. Wash your hands afterwards. Remember that the spray may harm pets, too.

If you do have a plant that looks unhealthy, put it by itself until it's better, or if it has a disease it may spread to other plants.

Red spider mite Look for brownish spotting on leaves or falling leaves, especially in summer. Bugs too tiny to see.

Scale insects Look for flat or rounded brown scales on both sides of leaves and on stem. Brush on methylated spirit.

Slugs, snails, worms, caterpillars Look for holes in leaves. These pests may get on your plants if they are outdoors in the summer for a while. Take off caterpillars by hand and free them outdoors. Spray other pests.

Look at your plants to see if they are healthy. If something is wrong, it may be from too much or too little water, light, humidity, heat or food.

Too much
Water Leaves turning yellow, falling, rotting or wilting in wet compost.
Buds falling.
Flowers falling.
Stems rotting.
Humidity Leaves growing grayish-colored mould.
Fungi or viruses showing (see p. 37).
Light Leaves turning brown round edges.
Heat Leaves wilting, turning brown around edges.
Food New stems or shoots growing weakly.

Mealy bug Look for white cotton-like covering on leaves and stems. Use methylated spirit. Throw out badly attacked plants.

Whitefly Look for leaves turning yellow. The insect lays eggs on undersides of leaves. Spray both flies and eggs.

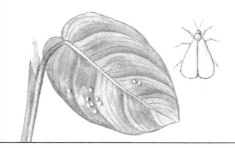

Aphids Look for pests on leaves and stems of all plants. The most common pests. Cause plants to grow out of shape. Spray.

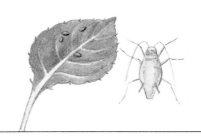

Cyclamen mite Look for curling leaves, rotting shoots and buds on Cyclamen, African Violet and Geraniums. Throw out plants.

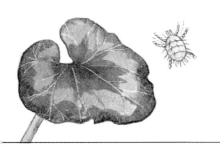

Fungi Look for spots on leaves. Cut off and throw away attacked leaves. Spray plant.

Viruses Look for light green patches on leaves. There is nothing to cure plants with viruses. Throw out plants.

Too Little
Water Leaves falling, wilting, growing small and dark. Buds falling. Flowers falling. Stems drooping.
Humidity Leaves wilting. Stems drooping.
Light Leaves growing out of shape and leaning towards light, green leaves turning yellow, variegated leaves losing marks. New stems or shoots growing weakly.
Heat Leaves turning brown around edges.
Food Leaves small, growing slowly. Flowers small, poorly colored. Stems growing slowly. Shoots growing slowly.

Plant chart

Name	Light	Water	Minimum winter temperature
Achimenes	indirect	well in summer, sparingly in spring and autumn	45°F
African Violet	shade	from below, keeping moist	60°F
Aluminum Plant	indirect	well in summer, moderately in winter	50°F
Amaryllis	p. 12	see p. 12	55°F
Asparagus Fern	indirect	well in summer, barely in winter	45°F
Begonia rex	shade	well April-Sept., moist in winter	55°F
Cape Primrose	shade	well in summer, moderately in winter	50°F
Cast Iron Plant	indirect	moderately in summer, less in winter	45°F
Chinese Hibiscus	direct	well in summer, moderately in winter	55°F
Christmas Cactus	indirect	well in winter, almost dry in summer	55°F
Chrysanthemum (short-day)	direct	well while flowering	50°F
Coleus	direct	well in summer, just moist in winter	55°F
Common Ivy	shade	moist all year	
Cyclamen	indirect	from bottom when growing, dry when resting	55°F
Daffodil	p. 12	see p. 12	
Date Palm	p. 14	well in spring and summer, sparingly in winter	50°F
Echeveria gibbiflora	direct	regularly in summer, barely in winter	40°F
Echinocereus pectinatus	direct	well in summer, dry Oct.-March	40°F
Golden Barrel	direct	moist in summer, dry Oct.-March	40°F
Hyacinth	p. 21	see p. 21	
Impatiens	p. 16	well in summer, moist in winter	50°F
Ivy-leaved Geranium	direct	regularly in summer, almost dry in winter	45°F
Jade Plant	direct	sparingly in summer, dry other times	40°F
Kangaroo Vine	indirect	well in summer, just moist in winter	45°F
Maidenhair Fern	shade	well in summer, just moist in winter	45°F
Partridge-breasted Aloe	direct	sparingly in summer, barely in winter	40°F
Philodendron	indirect	well in summer, moist other times	55°F
Piggy-back Plant	indirect	moist all year	35°F
Prayer Plant	shade	well in summer, sparingly in winter	55°F
Queen's Tears	shade	well May-Sept., just moist in winter	50°F
Rubber Tree	shade	well in summer, just moist in winter	50°F
Shrimp Plant	direct	well in summer, just moist in winter	45°F
Speedy Jenny	indirect	well in summer, moist in winter	50°F
Spider Plant	direct	well Feb.-Sept., sparingly Oct.-Jan.	45°F
Swiss Cheese Plant	indirect	well in summer, just moist in winter	50°F
Tulip	p. 12	see p. 12	
Urn Plant	indirect	see p. 18	50°F
Wandering Jew	indirect	well in summer, just moist in winter	45°F
Watermelon Peperomia	indirect	moderately in summer, just moist in winter	55°F
Weeping Fig	indirect	well in summer, just moist in winter	50°F

Propagation	Feeding	Repotting	Ease
separate tubers and repot	every 2 weeks spring-flowering	all-peat compost in spring	✸✸✸
leaf cuttings, division in spring	every 3 weeks in summer	all-peat compost	✸✸
tip cuttings early summer	every 2 weeks March-Sept.	April	✸
remove offsets	see p. 12	every second Oct., half-covered	✸
division in spring	every 2 weeks in summer	April	✸
leaf cuttings in summer, seeds	every 2 weeks April-Sept.	all-peat compost every April	✸✸
leaf cuttings in summer, seeds	every 2 weeks in summer	in shallow pot every March	✸
division in spring	once a month in summer	all-peat compost when needed	✸✸
cuttings	once a week Feb.-Aug.	all-peat compost in Feb.	✸
cuttings in summer	weekly when flower buds form	cactus compost	✸✸
see p. 10	none	none	✸✸
tip cuttings spring or summer	every 2 weeks April-Sept.	Feb.	✸
tip cuttings in autumn	once a month April-Sept.	every second Feb.	✸
seeds	every 2 weeks when flower buds	every Aug.	✸✸
none	none	none	✸
none	every 2 weeks May-Sept.	see p. 14	✸✸
leaf or stem cuttings in summer	once a month in summer	every 2 years in April	✸✸
stem cuttings in summer, seeds	once a month in summer	in compost and coarse sand	✸
seeds in spring	once a month March-Aug.	cactus compost	✸✸
none	none	none	✸
tip cuttings in summer, seeds	weekly in summer	all-peat compost in spring	✸✸✸
tip cuttings in summer	once a month April-Sept.	all-peat compost in spring	✸
leaf cuttings spring and summer	once a month April-July	every second April	✸
stem tip cuttings in summer	every 2 weeks April-Sept.	every second Feb.	✸
division in spring	once a month April-Sept.	all-peat compost in spring	✸
remove offsets in summer	every 2 weeks in March	every 2 years in spring	✸✸
stem tip cuttings in summer	every 2 weeks May-Sept.	every second spring	✸✸
plantlets or division of parent	once a week March-Sept.	all-peat compost in spring	✸
division in spring	every 2 weeks May-Sept.	every spring	✸✸✸
division in summer	every 2 weeks May-Sept.	all-peat compost in summer	✸✸
stem tip cuttings, air layering	every 2 weeks in summer	every second April	✸
stem tip cuttings in spring	every 2 weeks April-Sept.	March	✸
tip cuttings in summer	every 2 weeks April-Sept.	April	✸
plantlets any time	once a week Feb.-Sept.	spring	✸
stem tip cuttings in summer	every 2 weeks April-Sept.	every third April	✸✸
none	none	none	✸
see p. 18	once a month April-Oct.	see p. 18	✸✸
tip cuttings in spring	every 2 weeks April-Sept.	spring	✸
leaf cuttings in summer	once a month May-Sept.	April	✸✸
cuttings in summer	every 2 weeks May-Sept.	every second April	✸✸

Index

Latin names are in *italic*.
Page numbers in *italic* refer to illustrations.

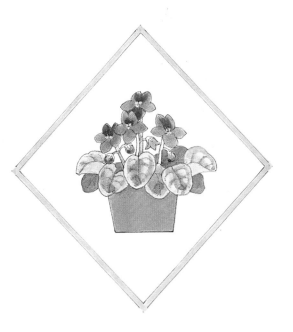